The Adventures of
Joy Girl

Joy Girl Loses a Pet

Patricia Y. Hunter

The Adventures of Joy Girl: Joy Girl Loses a Pet

© May 3, 2022

Patricia Hunter

Illustrations by: Silver Lining

ISBN# 978-1-953526-31-1

All rights reserved under international copyright law. This book or parts thereof may not be reproduced in any form, stored in a retrieval system, or transmitted in any form by any means; electronic, mechanical, photocopy, recording, or otherwise without prior written permission of the publisher or author, except as provided by United States of America copyright.

Published by TaylorMade Publishing
Jacksonville, FL
www.TaylorMadePublishingFL.com
(904) 323-1334

Introduction

Joy Girl was always out and about, spreading Joy to the world. She encouraged everyone she met. She lifted their spirits by singing "The Joy of the Lord is Your Strength," and "Joy, Joy, God's Great Joy."

One day, Joy's mother and father surprised her with a magnificent gift – her very own puppy. She had been asking them for one for a long time, but they told her she had to learn to be more responsible before she could get a pet. The day Joy Girl met her four-legged friend, her heart overflowed with Joy.

She had no idea that her Joyful heart would one day be broken, that she would be overcome by the unfamiliar emotion of grief when her pet died.

Grief is a natural emotional response resulting from a significant loss – especially the death of a loved one. Joy Girl's parents helped her learn how to walk through her grief, trusting God, until she came out on the other side.

Joy Girl was so happy when her parents finally got her a puppy.

She named him Sunny. She fed him, took him for walks, cuddled with him, and so much more.

They were best friends.

They became closer and closer
as the years went by.
If you saw Joy Girl,
you saw Sunny.

One day, Joy Girl let Sunny out for his morning routine, and he never returned.

Her dad went out to look for him. Dad found Sunny, but he was not alive.

Joy Girl's heart hurt so much. She became really sad for a very long time.

Her parents and friends were so concerned about her.

Joy Girl's sadness stopped her from spreading Joy to everyone, but she did not want to talk about why she was so hurt and sad.

Grief is a normal response to loss, but it is not healthy to keep the sad feelings inside.

Joy Girl felt like her entire world had been turned upside down.

She missed her best friend, Sunny, so much.

You have to learn to relate to the world without your loved one.

Joy Girl could not stop thinking about the morning that Sunny died. She cried every time the thought came up.

Her family and friends told her they missed her JOYFULNESS. They did not like it when she was sad and angry.

When you lose a loved one,
the last moments of their life
sometimes replay over and
over in your mind like a scene from a movie.

Joy Girl tried so hard to get back to her normal self.

She prayed to God her Father, asking Him for strength to get through this difficult time.

God reminded Joy Girl that her strength comes from Him.

It is normal to feel exhausted
- physically, emotionally, and spiritually
- when grieving.

Her mother made her favorite meals and desserts for dinner, but Joy Girl did not feel hungry.

She also had a hard time falling asleep. Joy Girl did not understand what was going on with her.

When grieving, your appetite and sleep patterns may change. You may not feel like yourself for a moment. But it does get better.

Joy Girl did not recognize who she had become.

She had been drained of her Joy and peace.

You may have days where you feel like you do not recognize yourself. The things that you once enjoyed, you may not enjoy anymore.

Some days she could feel Joy, unspeakable Joy.

Then, out of nowhere, the Joy disappeared, and she felt sad and lonely again.

You may start to feel better and then suddenly be hit by a wave of sadness.

Joy Girl knew she did not want to feel like this forever. Sunny would want her to be JOYOUS again.

But she did not want to feel like she had forgotten about him.

It is healthy to be able to experience life again and to be able to live with the great memories of your loved one. It is okay to find yourself not thinking about your loss as much as time goes by. This does not mean you are forgetting your loved one.

Joy Girl noticed she was beginning to enjoy the things that she loved again.

This was her prayer, to feel like Joy Girl again.

She started spending time with friends and family.

At first, Joy Girl had a hard time talking about her furry friend.

But she learned that talking about him made her smile and laugh at the precious memories.

It could be hard to talk about your lost loved one at first. But hopefully, time will heal those wounds.

Joy Girl began to heal.

She started loving on people again and sharing Joy with them.

Some days she had to push herself toward Joy, and when she did, the grief became easier.

It is important not to let grief last too long, because it could lead to other health issues.

Joy Girl talked with her parents about her feelings.

They prayed for her during her time of sorrow, and her hope and peace were restored.

She started to feel like she may want another fur baby in the future.

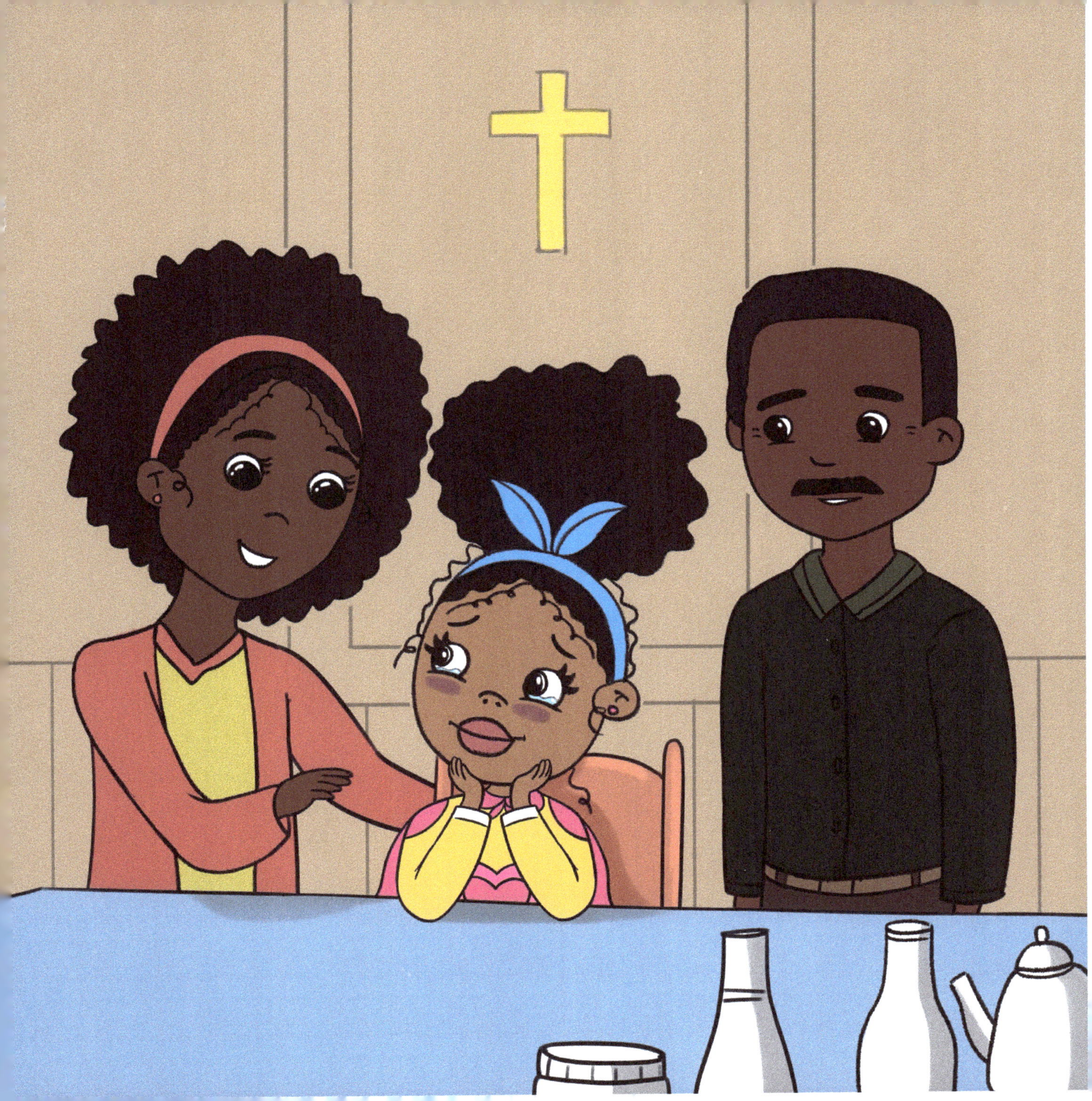

When she felt her joy decreasing, Joy Girl reached out to God, and He rescued her.

"Peace I leave with you, my peace I give unto you..." John 14:27

"...The Joy of the Lord is your strength." Nehemiah 8:10

Talk to your parents about your feelings.

If your grief is too hard for you,

you may need professional help.

About the Author
Patricia Yvette Hunter

As a young adult, Mrs. Hunter realized that she wanted to influence the lives of young people in the educational arena. Her passion and her deep desire to assist students, both academically and mentally, was obvious early in her career as an elementary educator.

Mrs. Hunter served as an elementary educator from 1996-2006. She honored her calling to educate the whole child by returning to college for her master's degree in counseling. She graduated from Florida Agricultural and Mechanical University with a bachelor's degree in elementary education and a master's degree in school counseling and obtained her mental health licensure from Webster University. She is highly regarded by her peers in the fields of education and counseling.

Along with working as an elementary educator, she has also worked as a school counselor and a military student support specialist. Additionally, she is a certified youth mental health first aid instructor and a licensed mental health counselor. She has been in private practice for 2 years and is currently a mental health counselor with Clay County Schools. Her expertise in the field of counseling has landed her multiple appearances in print magazines, on local news segments, and Clay County school district news.

Mrs. Hunter works with children from a variety of academic levels and socio-economic statuses. Although out of the day-to-day classroom, she continues to assist a small roster of students achieve academic success. In her ongoing support of parents and students who have experienced trauma, Mrs. Hunter helps students access mental health services and social-emotional assistance when needed. She is actively involved in her church, serving as a youth leader. Her desire to educate and assist the whole child is reflected in all that she does.

Personally, Mrs. Hunter is married to the love of her life, Forrest Hunter. Mr. Hunter is the epitome of a supportive husband and applauds his wife's passion to make every child she encounters, whole. She has a son who is a graduate of Florida State University. Mrs. Hunter enjoys spending her free time with her loving family and friends. This book was written in loving memory of her sweet fur baby, Bear.